IT HAPPENED

Your Hands-Your Kiss-Your Love

CLIANDA FLORENCE

Book Coach – Robin Devonish
Cover Design – Bookney
Editing and Layout – Pen Publish Profit™
Interior Design – www.queekpub.com
Editor: CaTyra Polland   polland@love4words.com
ISBN 13: 979-8-9864269-1-4
LCCN: 2022916236
Printed in the United States of America

ACKNOWLEDGMENTS

To Robin Devonish and CaTyra Polland, I want to thank both you Sis-Stars for your hard work and guidance throughout this amazing journey.

Thank you, my beautiful, talented, artistic cousin Alanna Nelson for your artistic design.

To my friends and family that listened and critiqued my work along the way I thank you.

To my dear friend and mentor Sis. Dicker you always told me to tell my story and put it on paper. I didn't believe I had much to say, but now I have the Strength 2 Say what's on my heart. Thank you for watching over me in heaven.

DEDICATION

This book of poetry is dedicated to a person who saw me without touching me. The person who showed me what a real man is and looks like. The man who made passionate love to my mind, creating curiosity, wonder, and peace. To the one who has reached down to the essence of my Soul, who has created a space for organic agape love, the Love that only comes from God. This form of love is rare, when you experience it, you walk, talk, think, and smile differently. You feel things you never imagined, you become lost for words! It's at that point "It Happens" , you better put on your seat belt for the ride of your life.

CONTENTS

LEARNING 2 BE!

When I sat down and began this journey, I went through so many emotions because I was about to pour parts of myself on paper that many did not know about. Throughout the writing process, I became empowered and encouraged to Be!

BE…

Confident

Sexy

Bold

Courageous

Adventurous

ME!

I hope that as you read these poems it awakens parts of you that have been dormant or not existed due to fear. Many people have a misconception that one who is God-fearing, professional, and classy in the street cannot be a freak in the sheets. Many people struggle because of dull sex lives. We can become other people in the bedroom. Sex is an expression; like an artist you use an assortment of colors, textures, and tools. When you experience a true connection that transcends the physical, your sexual experience will flourish. When one truly understands what intimacy is, feels, and looks like you will have explosive lovemaking. When you and your mate are into one another, your sexual experience will be both fulfilling and mind-blowing. When you feel good about yourself and your body you will not walk in fear: you will explode in ecstasy because of mutual love and respect.

Learning to "BE" at times can be difficult and challenging. There are so many voices in society that get in the way of how you see yourself. Once you walk in acceptance knowing who you are, you will "BE":

Bold

Caring

Confident

Daring

Demanding

Loving

Learning to "BE" is a journey! Be patient with yourself; push yourself to work on one or two things about yourself at a time. Be willing to learn new things about yourself. At times while on your road to becoming you must open your mind to new possibilities. Make time for yourself and be willing to do the WORK. Once you do, trust me your sexual experience will be mind-blowing and fulfilling because you have learned to BE YOU.

IF I WERE...

If I were your woman, I would pray over you in the morning as I watch you sleep asking God to guide you and keep you.

Thanking Him for creating you just for me!

Showering to wake you pleasing you with my mouth sucking you nice and slow. Sit on top of you while gazing into your eyes telling you why I love you without a word coming forth from my mouth!

Sit at your feet and learn from you take in all the wisdom you hold.

Creating space for you to continue to sharpen your sword. Standing by your side as you do the work within the church & community.

If I were your woman and you were my man, I would meet you at noon with a jacket and heels with nothing on to show you what to expect when you come home.

Shower you with so much love and affection so you know and understand when you go out 50 women could step to you, but you know without a shadow of a doubt that your WIFE has everything you both desire and need!

If I were your woman and you were my man, I would thank God for allowing us to experience a piece of Heaven on Earth!

If I Were...

THE ENCOUNTER

You jumped out so I'm jumping back at you. Following your lead; I trust you to go ahead of me walking in my mind, in my dreams. I've seen you before, sometimes right next to me, but do you notice me?

I have watched you from afar, love your intelligence, your love for God, the way you command a room with such grace. I wonder does he even know.?

It is what it is, I'm going out on a limb; It's time to step to him and tell him my deep feelings that lie inside.

He walks by, I become shy, so I send a simple text "Wish I had some Starbucks."

YOUR TOUCH

I can't explain how I feel, gazing at you from afar
wondering how your touch would be.

Your words have already found their way to the hidden
places of my heart and mind that I've kept guarded for
so long.

I shared with you my past hurt, pain, and shame.

You touched my lips, looked into my eyes, and said, "It's
time for something new.

Your Soul called out to me; it led me to you."

My mind is racing; my God this man captures me.

His hand ran across my face, I closed my eyes, the pure
passion of peace!

Just like that, the touch of his lips on mine.

OUR FIRST KISS!!!!!

I'M VERY PRIVATE & GUARDED

You saw me in a room, I caught your eye, you walked by touched the small of my back, and said hi.

Wanting to get close to you, to touch you again. You came out where I was to sit, to hear, to say so much, and know it's our special private place. I asked if you could meet my needs. Your reply caught my eye, nearly taking my breath away.

"That's what I'm trained to do!"

Do you think you can handle me was what came to mind? The way he whispered in my ear

"of course,"

got my Sweet Box wet, dripping down my legs.

TAKE EM TO BRAZIL

I'm getting wet at the thought of your voice, your hand touching my face, your words in my ear bouncing off my eardrum!

What is a girl to do? I imagine your hands and face going places.

Your lips touching both pairs of mine.

You send me on a natural high. Man, she needs to answer this line.

I need to schedule a Brazilian for this Man of mine.

She doesn't understand he loves to eat, to taste my sweet box that's juicy as a peach.

He does something to me.

I want to please him and cum all over his lips. I just love how he catches each drip. It's about that time for our exotic trip to Brazil.

PURPLE RAIN

Like the raindrops from the sky, I want your words and body to fall on me.

Purple means royalty and it fits.

Our favorite color: the light and dark hues are just as captivating as you.

You have painted a Masterpiece in my mind; my Soul has taken a hold of you.

You embrace me and just like that, I become wet.

You glide your hands between my thighs, you gaze into my eyes.

You kiss my lips and whisper "Rain down on me. I want to see your secret garden.

I want to read your mind, know your deepest feelings."

What am I to do? He commands my body in ways no other has done.

The passion is so strong and real. I want him to feel what I feel.

I want to dance in the rain, just me and you.

THAT'S WHAT A MAN SUPPOSED TO DO

I thank him for his kind gestures, I'm met with

"Don't thank me for anything I do, that's what a Man Supposed to Do"

That statement stopped me dead in my tracks. Gripping my face so gentle with his hands gazing into my eyes he softly said,

"I don't know who you dealt with before, but he was not a real man; he was intimidated by you leaving you uncovered. That will never happen with me.

I just ask one thing of you, please don't hurt me. Like you, many have taken advantage of me."

My heart and mind are racing, I'm lost for words, I look him in his eyes and tell him he is safe with me, that's what a woman is supposed to do.

We kiss, embrace as my heart touches his chest. He says so soft and sweet,

"You will never be left uncovered again!"

MY SWEET ADDICTION

Growing up never would I imagine becoming addicted to anything,

but this man is like a drug.

Slapping my arm feeling him deep in my veins.

What's happening to me; his Soul is taking hold of me.

I shake when he leaves going through withdrawals.

Nothing physical outside of a kiss.

What is coming over me? He is entering me nice and slow.

I'm going to have a fit.

He calls, I light up.

When I see him, he wraps his arms around me so tight.

I need him to truly feel me.

I unzip his pants and place him in my mouth nice and slow.

As I look up at him, his eyes are closed; head back, he says my name in a way that grabs me.

It's at that point

I verified I was not alone; he's addicted too!

FINE & FLY

"Come on out so I can watch you walk,"

he says over the phone.

This man does something to me.

I feel like a girl in high school who has a crush.

He's such a gentleman; I love the way he smells. He embraces me; I'm captivated.

I stand in suspense asking myself what it's like to be in love.

The sound of water and birds; the perfect spot.

I look over to the left and imagine us laying on a blanket talking, kissing like the scene from Jason's Lyric.

He kisses me and asks, "Are you with me?"

Of course, just images of us caught up in my mind. He spins me around and says:

"You're so fine and fly!"

CHANGING FACES

This Man has truly fallen from Heaven, created just for me.

He does something each time I see him.

I become lost for words can't help but become shy causing my face to change.

Can't look him in the face, biting my lips, running each time the phone rings.

He enjoys seeing me like this.

I can't lie I love this feeling; his words display across my phone through text, which causes me heart to skip a beat.

He calls I come; I call he makes things happen.

I absolutely love the change in me. My heart is dancing; I prayed for a Man like this!

I WONDER...

I had to go out of town, we both thought of one another.

You pulled me in, then hit me with "I wonder what a trip with you would be like?" That messed me up because I began to daydream, waking up in Costa Rica on a black sand beach.

Going on walks, making love in the sand kissing you nice and slow as you wrap your arms around me.

As the waves hit our bodies, I cause you to lose your mind as I suck you slow;

not to be outdone, you lay me on my back beginning to kiss me, going down to my sweet box, causing me to explode as you enter.

We eat dinner, talk having deep stimulating conversations. You say "hello" three times; I snap back to reality.

I WONDER...

THE ONLY THING MISSING...

The beauty of time, affords one the opportunity to reflect, chill, learn, grow, and glow. I thought I experienced love before, not realizing it was counterfeit.

This man has shown me things at 40 I've never experienced.

He is not drawn to my body, but my Mind, my Spirit, my Intelligence, my Soul, the very essence of me!

He captivates me, but I'm scared of hurt and pain. He is so in tune; before I even found the words he said "You don't have to worry about me hurting you. Trust God, turn that page, heal and begin to focus on the new thing God will do with and through you!"

My mouth drops: he is so right that at times I find myself rereading words he has said! He has become the missing link; I was not even searching for!

I DON'T DO THE EXPECTED

"Maybe because I don't do the expected when it's expected…because I'm special and unique."

I was subdued, once again lost for words!

Mentally he has me taking trips; his smile captivates me.

To do the unexpected is truly who he is at his core.

He's meticulous when it comes to me each time blowing my mind, leaving me in earnest expectation of what he will do next.

This man takes me places, allowing me to see things I never imagined

He is a true doer, a man of few words; when he does speak the meaning goes so deep that it grabs me, takes hold of me doing things I never expected.

Oh yes, he does the unexpected very well.

I FEEL...

Safe with you

Renewed

Encouraged

Inspired

Energized

Shy

Love ALL Over Me

Sexy

Empowered

My Voice

Pregnant with new potential & possibilities

Strength

Joy

Like I can walk on water

Protected

Sad when you're not near me

Like I Found MY SOUL MATE!

WITH EARNEST EXPECTATION

I can't get you off my mind as I look forward to your embrace and as I kiss your face.

Each time I close my eyes I, imagining what it's going to be like when we make love. The passion that lies within is mind-blowing.

The love that I have runs deep as I want you in me. I can hear you saying how much you love me and need me as much as I need you.

A soul tie something one often desires, but never in a million years did I think that would be You & I. You are so rare and precious.

I need to hold you close feeling every part of you.

Taking it slow, pleasing one another. If you only knew how long I've waited to experience real love & passion.

With earnest expectation, I wait patiently for you!

A REAL MAN

When encountering a real man, it does something to you!

It causes you to fix your crown, dust yourself off, no longer dimming your shine.

You put sunglasses on me, not intimidated or afraid of my shine.

I want to pull you close, kiss you, please you because I want to be yours.

My desire is for you to learn and explore all the intricate parts of me, the beauty, and the scars because I feel safe with you, knowing you will protect me from harm.

A real woman looks for protection and provision from her man I see that in you! The way you said

"I will have my secretary take care of you" caused me to view you differently.

My father has been the only other man that has covered me in such a way.

It's been hard to feel and express my true feelings, but you have done something to me.

You have figured out the beat to my drum, the dope verse over a tight beat.

You are truly special to me.

PARTS OF ME

You have awakened parts of me I thought could never be

You take me places mentally

You paint pictures in my mind with your words

You have a way of gazing into me while seeing yet never entering me

When I don't speak to you or see you, I feel an absence, a void that only you can fill

While in your presence, I become shy

You have a way of calming me with each word and touch

Your kiss subdues me in ways I never imagined

You make me want to love again, something I vowed I'd never do again due to past hurt

I'm stepping out my comfort zone, showing you love in ways I never imagined

I've become excited at the very thought of you

My desire to please you while keeping a smile on your face and heart

NEEDING YOU

I need you in so many ways
You don't know
You take me places
I'm so afraid to go
I'm excited
I feel alive again
I
Love how you are with me
We can move
From being
Hommie
Lovers
And
Friends
We can talk
Business
And switch the tempo
To
Your dick hitting the back of my throat
And

Gripping your desk as you taste and stroke so
intentionally with passion

I love

Gazing into your eyes

Your smile

Your touch

Your embrace is so refreshing & new

At times

I fight back tears

I can't believe these feelings are real & true

I'm falling

In

Love with you!

I REMEMBER

Basking in the love and newness of me, grateful for your care How you surrendered to the intense passion of lovemaking that was both fulfilling & mind blowing

Remembering the hurt I experienced for six-years fighting with my worth asking myself what more could I do to be seen

For my cries to be noticed

For years I settled not wanting to fail

The love you covered me with helped me see I'm perfectly & wonderfully made

I desire to be

Admired, loved, cherished & sexy

I never thought I would experience what I did with you

As I lie in the same place you kissed me

Made passionate love to me

My eyes fill with tears

I have so many feelings stirring up in me

You have awakened me in ways that no one ever has

To be covered by a real man who loves God is something I can't easily put into words

I no longer want to recall the hurt of my past

I now have a renewed strength to see me

Her beauty

Power

Freaky side

Voice

I have a new song in my heart

To be catered to is something so beautiful & new

This is what I will always remember

A real man now knows the beat of my drum who has
elevated my thinking & being

Someone I connect with that transcends the physical

Your soft lips with each kiss has renewed me

Your embrace has drawn me into a safe place to become
vulnerable

To let down my guard, allowing you in spaces and places
I never knew existed

I remember the first time I saw you from afar wondering,

Seeing you again curious,

Talking to you feeling so comfortable

Kissing you

Feeling passion

Wanting to learn more

I remember

Do you?

SOUL VS. BODY

Someone once said, "find you someone who will love your soul more than your body!"

The very essence of who you are

The good, bad, & ugly

That someone who will never do what one of Noah's children did when he was drunk looking upon him when he was exposed and vulnerable; but like the son who walked backwards covering him up. A real man is going to cover you not expose you to the harmful elements of life. When you feel that you're willing to respect him the way God commands, it is through that genuine respect

You show love

Loving the body is just the surface, what happens when it changes when you let one another down? If there is no soul tie, you will walk away very easily! When I think of one who completes you it's something special, rare, and only comes once in a lifetime

Someone who you can be yourself with, challenges you, and covers you. Someone who can fuck your brains out and make passionate love to you in ways unimaginable. Someone who matches your intelligence and causes you to think differently

When they are not there, they still are.

A true soul tie will awaken parts of you that you thought could never be done. They will take you places mentally, paint pictures in your mind with their words.

You can look into one another and see without entering physically. When you don't talk or see one each other you feel a way. When you see him, you become shy.

He subdues you with his presence, voice, and touch

His kiss calm you in ways you never imagined. When you make love, it brings tears to your eyes. You become excited, wanting to please him and he you because you both are speaking to the essence of who you are.

YOUR SOUL MATE

You have my body weak

I'm all smiles

Body craving you and your touch

anticipating seeing you and hearing about your
experiences

I love how you handle and investigate me

You have shown me what real intimacy looks and feels
like

Into me you have seen, and I feel amazing

I feel like I'm on a roller coaster; I don't want to get off

A high I never want to come down from

The remnants of your kiss lay across my lips; I can still
taste you

A song of love plays down to my Soul

You have stepped in; I'm no longer afraid to get wet by
life's rain

Drunk in love you and me

A love that will last for eternity

I LOVE

The way you slide into my mouth and hit the back of my throat

How you slide across my lips

The way you feel in my hands, making love to you with my mouth is no chore

To witness the way your eyes close and your head goes back does something to me

I feel like I'm in ecstasy; I have such a strong desire to please you in every way

I desire to feel all of you in my mouth and each wet place

I enjoy watching you with each stroke, stopping and kissing you

Tasting your lips and drops of your cologne on my tongue turns me one once again

I want to capture each breath as a photographer does with each shot

Hoping I get the opportunity to take a portion of you with me

I look forward to you letting go, releasing in my mouth and swallow

Showing you how into you I am

I desire to please you and only you!

I CAN

Taste you in my mouth

Smell your cologne but you're nowhere to be found

I can feel you without touching you

The thoughts of you cause me to climax

Wait for you because no one can match

Love you like no other

See into you, as you see into me

Kiss you as I gaze into your eyes grinding on you nice
and slow as you rub your hands all over me

WHAT HAVE YOU DONE TO ME?

MISSING YOU ALREADY

I pray you are safe

I want to be your peace during your storms

I want to hold you and shield you from the rain of life

I want to speak life into the places where you are weak
and broken

I desire to hold you in my arms, hugging you, kissing you
while we gaze into one another's eyes

I want to feel you and hear you whisper in my ear

Remembering you as we lay together and you recite
vows to me, asking me questions

Running back in my mind when you first told me this is
irrevocable, not believing you

I now understand as I face the dim reality of not seeing
you for a week

I desire to see you grow, becoming who God has destined
you to be

I want to be a part of your elevation; I want to upgrade
you

This, I believe is what I was created to do

I thank God for placing you in my life; I see and feel
things so differently now

I have found new strength and outlook on life

You have spoiled me

You got me like this

I can go on and on

You already know what it is

I LOVE YOU

THE WAY

I love you

I adore you

I breathe you

I miss your touch

The way you investigate me

My body is calling

You have the key

I'm waiting for you to touch down

Anticipating when you will lay me down like a prayer

Running your hands everywhere

I can see you now stepping back admiring me

Sizing me up as you lick your lips

Spreading my legs

Kissing and licking my inner thighs

You send me on a natural high

You kiss my second set of lips

As you softly slide your fingers inside

The sound of you sucking drives me wild

The way you write your name in it with a sense of
urgency

You stop, say my name, commanding my body to cum to you

As you slide inside

Our bodies instantly connect

As you whisper in my ear

It's time cum to me the way I like it

I explode!